THÉRÈSE RAQUIN

a play by

Neal Bell

adapted from the novel by
Emile Zola

BROADWAY PLAY PUBLISHING INC
56 E 81st St., NY NY 10028-0202
212 772-8334 fax: 212 772-8358
http://www.BroadwayPlayPubl.com

THÉRÈSE RAQUIN
© Copyright 1998 by Neal Bell

First printing: April 1998
ISBN: 0-88145-136-3

Book design: Marie Donovan
Word processing: Microsoft Word for Windows
Typographic controls: Xerox Ventura Publisher 2.0 PE
Typeface: Palatino
Copy editing: Liam Brosnahan
Printed on recycled acid-free paper and bound in the USA

ABOUT THE AUTHOR

Mr Bell's plays—including TWO SMALL BODIES, RAW YOUTH, COLD SWEAT, READY FOR THE RIVER, SLEEPING DOGS, RAGGED DICK, ON THE BUM, and SOMEWHERE IN THE PACIFIC—have appeared at Playwrights Horizons in New York and at regional theatres including the Berkeley Rep, the Mark Taper Forum, South Coast Rep, the La Jolla Playhouse, and Actors Theatre of Louisville, where his ten-minute play OUT THE WINDOW was a co-winner of the 1990 Heideman Award. Mr Bell has been a playwright-in-residence at the Yale Drama School, and has taught playwriting at New York University, Playwrights Horizons Theatre School, and the 42nd Street Collective. A recipient of fellowships from the Rockefeller Foundation, the National Endowment and the Guggenheim Foundation, Mr Bell was awarded an Obie Award in 1992 for sustained achievement in playwriting.

ORIGINAL PRODUCTIONS

THÉRÈSE RAQUIN was first produced at New York University, under the auspices of the Playwrights Horizons Theatre School. It opened on 3 December 1991 and featured the following cast and creative contributors:

MADAME .... Katie Doyle-Ekert
CAMILLE .... Chris Diana
THÉRÈSE .... Katie Bainbridge
LAURENT.......................... Jake Beecham
GRIVET .... Evan Miller
MICHAUD .... Gregg Mulpagano
OLIVIER .... Josh Appel
SUZANNE .... Heather Koenig

Director .... Edward Elefterion
Sets .... Jeremy Cable
Costumes .... Shawnee Summer
Lighting .... John Chiappa
Stage manager .... Heidi Epsha

THÉRÈSE RAQUIN received its first professional production at the Williamstown Theatre Festival. It opened on 30 June 1993 and featured the following cast and creative contributors:

MADAME .... Beth Dixon
CAMILLE .... Todd Weeks
THÉRÈSE .... Lynn Hawley
LAURENT .... Garret Dillahunt
GRIVET .... Adam Stein
MICHAUD .... Charles Fisher
OLIVIER .... Billy Rosenfeld
SUZANNE .... Laura D Arista

Director .... Michael Greif
Sets .... Betsy McDonald
Costumes .... Deanna Berg
Lights .... Betsy Finston
Sound .... Rob Smith
Stage manager .... Sally Plass

The West Coast premiere of THÉRÈSE RAQUIN was produced by the La Jolla Playhouse, La Jolla, California (Des McAnuff, Artistic Director; Terrence Dwyer, Managing Director), opening on 10 July 1994 with the following cast and creative contributors:

MADAME .... Beth Dixon
CAMILLE .... Paul Giamatti
THÉRÈSE ....Angie Phillips
LAURENT.............................David Hunt
GRIVET ....Kent Davis
MICHAUD .... Tony Amedola
OLIVIER ....Silas Weir Mitchell
SUZANNE .... Laurie Williams

Director .... Michael Greif
Scenic design ....Marina Draghici
Costume design ....Mark Wendland
Lighting design .... Kenneth Posner
Sound design .... Nathan Birnbaum
Dramaturgy .... Robert Blacker

THÉRÈSE RAQUIN had its professional New York premiere at the Classic Stage Company (David Esbjornson, Artistic Director; Mary Esbjornson, Executive Director) on 21 October 1997. The cast and creative contributors were:

MADAME .... Beth Dixon
CAMILLE .... Todd Weeks
THÉRÈSE .... Elizabeth Marvel
LAURENT .... Sean Haberle
GRIVET .... Ed Hodson
MICHAUD .... Clement Fowler
OLIVIER .... Steven Rattazzi
SUZANNE .... Angela Reed

Director .... David Esbjornson
Sets .... Narelle Sissons
Costumes .... Kaye Voyce
Lights .... Christopher Akerlind
Stage manager .... Amy Patricia Stern
Sound design and composition .... Rinde Eckert &
                                        Gina Leishman

CHARACTERS

MADAME
THÉRÈSE
CAMILLE
MICHAUD
OLIVIER
SUZANNE
GRIVET
LAURENT

The play begins in the countryside outside of Paris, and then moves to the city.

Late 1800s

ACT ONE

Scene One

(1)

(MADAME *and* THÉRÈSE)

(MADAME *is embroidering.* THÉRÈSE *is sitting and looking out.)*

MADAME: Thérèse. THÉRÈSE.

THÉRÈSE: Hmm...

MADAME: What is that sound you're making?

THÉRÈSE: Oh. I think the river goes like this....
(She hums a snatch of song.)

MADAME: Brooks babble, dear. But rivers don't go like anything. Do they?

THÉRÈSE: Yes. Like this. *(She hums again.)* Don't you hear?

MADAME: I hear your cousin coughing away.

THÉRÈSE: Below the coughing. Listen...

MADAME: I hear your cousin gasping for breath.

THÉRÈSE: Under the gasping. Auntie, please—

MADAME: I hear this house. This house is creaking as badly as I am. None of us gets any younger, dear.

THÉRÈSE: I hear the river.

MADAME: What a queer child.

(The tea-kettle whistles.)

MADAME: Is that what you heard?
The tea-kettle? Silly.

(THÉRÈSE and her aunt now speak together; THÉRÈSE is mocking the words she knows by heart.)

THÉRÈSE & MADAME: I think your cousin might like some tea. He drinks it all if *you* make it, Thérèse.

THÉRÈSE: *(To herself)* I think my cousin would like to get out of his sick-bed, Auntie, and kick his sour old sick-clothes off, and run up and down the dark hallways yelling, "God-damnable hell!" And then run for the river, stark naked, and jump on a barge. And sail away. I think my cousin would like some air.

MADAME: What's that?

THÉRÈSE: It's not *fair*.

MADAME: God gives and He takes away, Thérèse. God took away Camille's health. And gave him you. *(She holds her embroidery up.)* Do you like it?

(THÉRÈSE reads the embroidered message out loud;)

THÉRÈSE: "Don't make a sound. Keep quiet."

(2)

(THÉRÈSE and CAMILLE)

(THÉRÈSE is looking out the window.)

CAMILLE: What are you doing?

THÉRÈSE: Watching the river.

(Pause)

CAMILLE: Why?

(3)

(THÉRÈSE *is in the yard.* CAMILLE *approaches.*)

THÉRÈSE: Should you be out?

CAMILLE: I escaped. What is that smell?

THÉRÈSE: The lilacs.

CAMILLE: Oh.

THÉRÈSE: And someone haying across the river.
And probably me. I must have run all the way home.
In the sun. *(Pause)* Kiss me, Camille.

CAMILLE: Like this?

THÉRÈSE: No.

CAMILLE: Like this?

THÉRÈSE: No.

CAMILLE: How?

THÉRÈSE: Never mind.

(Pause)

CAMILLE: I bet I can knock you down.

THÉRÈSE: Don't try.

CAMILLE: I think I could.

THÉRÈSE: I think you'd be sorry.

(CAMILLE *wrestles briefly with* THÉRÈSE. *She throws him to
the ground.*)

CAMILLE: Thérèse?

THÉRÈSE: What?

CAMILLE: You look like a bear.

THÉRÈSE: How would you know?

CAMILLE: I saw one once at the zoo. A long time ago.

(MADAME *enters, appalled.*)

MADAME: Get off the damp ground! You'll catch your death! Mouth open! (*She whips out a spoon and a bottle.*)

CAMILLE: No.

MADAME: Thérèse will have some, won't you, darling?

(THÉRÈSE *screws up her face and swallows a spoonful.*)

MADAME: Now, be as brave as your cousin, you terrible boy.

(CAMILLE *takes his medicine, wincing.*)

MADAME: And come inside this *instant.* Look. The fog is rolling in off the river.

(MADAME *exits.*)

THÉRÈSE: You know how many elixirs and nostrums and tonics I've had to take? Since I first came to live with you? And I'm not sick. I'M NOT SICK! I'M NOT!

(*She runs off as* CAMILLE *watches her go.*)

(4)

(THÉRÈSE *is staring out the window.*)

(MADAME *and* CAMILLE *observe her.*)

MADAME: What is she doing?

CAMILLE: Watching the river.

MADAME: She thinks the river talks.

CAMILLE: I know.

MADAME: What does she think it says?

CAMILLE: Thérèse? What does the river say?

THÉRÈSE: "Don't make a sound. Keep quiet."

CAMILLE: The river says that? My mother says that.

MADAME: What? I say what?

CAMILLE: "Don't make a sound. Keep quiet."

MADAME: So you can keep sleeping.

CAMILLE: I'm tired of sleeping.

MADAME: You need your rest.

CAMILLE: I need eight hours. Not eighteen years!

MADAME: "How sharper than a serpent's tooth..."

THÉRÈSE: *(To* CAMILLE*)* Do you dream?

CAMILLE: Of course I dream. I've had to do something, all these cooped-up years.

MADAME: I'm dizzy. Thérèse—my salts.

THÉRÈSE: What do you dream?

CAMILLE: I dream about going to work, if the truth be known.

MADAME: Does it have to?

THÉRÈSE: Going to work?

CAMILLE: In some vast concern. At my own little desk. With a pair of crisp shirt-garters around my sleeves. And I'd balance a pen behind my ear. And get so bushed by the end of the day that I'd sleep without dreaming at all. And all around me, while I was working, the air would thrum with the hum of commerce. Can't you almost hear it now?

MADAME: I can't.

CAMILLE: Well, neither can I. Not here, in the madding countryside. Which is why we are moving to Paris. Next month.

MADAME: To Paris?

CAMILLE: Right after I marry Thérèse. As you always planned.

MADAME: As I planned?

CAMILLE: I have let you coddle me all of my life. The least you can do at this point is allow me a will of my own. Don't act so stunned.

MADAME: Stunned?

CAMILLE: You must have had dreams.

MADAME: I don't remember.

CAMILLE: When you were married.

MADAME: So long ago.

CAMILLE: Thérèse has dreams.

MADAME: What does she dream about?

THÉRÈSE: Cotton-wool. Rooms and rooms of cotton-wool.

(5)

(MADAME *and* THÉRÈSE, *who's holding a candle*)

MADAME: Can't you sleep?

THÉRÈSE: The moon is so bright. It woke me up.

MADAME: You mustn't be frightened. You don't even have to change your name. Tonight is your final night as Thérèse Raquin. Tomorrow you're Madame Camille Raquin. That's all there is to it.

THÉRÈSE: That's all.

MADAME: And at night, when you get to the top of the stairs, you'll turn to the left. Instead of the right.

(Pause)

THÉRÈSE: Auntie? You said you'd tell me—when I was married—where I came from.

MADAME: Under a cabbage leaf.

THÉRÈSE: Don't tease. You promised to tell. Who am I?

(Pause)

MADAME: My brother was an officer. He went away to sea. He met someone, somewhere, somehow, and brought you home. And died.

THÉRÈSE: Of a broken heart?

MADAME: Of malaria.

THÉRÈSE: Tell me more.

MADAME: That's all I know.

THÉRÈSE: Was my mother a princess?

MADAME: I'm sure I don't know. Do you think you have princess's blood?

(THÉRÈSE shakes her head, and softly sings to herself:)

THÉRÈSE: "My brother was an officer,
He went away to sea
He met someone, somewhere, somehow,
And brought you home to me—"
(She breaks off, looking out.)
Look how the moonlight makes the hills go gray...

MADAME: Will you miss this place?

THÉRÈSE: The river, yes.

MADAME: We were happy here. In the quiet. I know. But I think we'll be happier yet. I do. I've found the most wonderful shop to rent, with three beautiful rooms above an enthralling arcade.... We'll fill the windows with treasures of haberdashery, and people

will simply beat down a wide path to our door.
And we'll live like queens in exile.

THÉRÈSE: Will we?

MADAME: So say goodbye to the hills and the river.
And come to bed.

THÉRÈSE: The river can't talk.

MADAME: But you think it can.

(MADAME *exits.* THÉRÈSE *looks out.*)

THÉRÈSE: I know it can.

(THÉRÈSE *hums to herself as the lights fade.*)

Scene Two

(1)

(MADAME, CAMILLE, *and* THÉRÈSE *are entering the new shop they've bought in Paris.*)

CAMILLE: "I've found the most wonderful shop,"
you said.

MADAME: I saw it in daylight, of course....

CAMILLE: "An enthralling arcade..."

MADAME: It *was* enthralling, with customers bustling
up and down—

CAMILLE: "Three beautiful rooms"...

MADAME: I *adore* this flat.

CAMILLE: It's smaller than you said.

MADAME: A bit.

CAMILLE: It's damp.

MADAME: Is it? It seems quite dry.

CAMILLE: It's dark—

MADAME: It's night! Be fair. When the sun streams down...

CAMILLE: It's mean.

MADAME: It's dirty. All it needs is sweeping, dear.

CAMILLE: Thérèse?

THÉRÈSE: Hmm?

CAMILLE: What do you think?

THÉRÈSE: It's narrow.

MADAME: *Cozy*, say.

THÉRÈSE: It's cold. It smells like newly turned earth.

MADAME: *(Sniffing)* Does it?

CAMILLE: I myself will be cooped up tight at the office all day. And you two girls will have each other to thin the gloom. And customers bustling in and out.... Thérèse?

THÉRÈSE: What?

CAMILLE: Will it do?

(THÉRÈSE *sits on her stool, assuming the pose we saw in the very beginning.*)

MADAME: Not even to mention the wonders I know we can work, with flowers at all the windows, and wallpaper—
flocked, I think—perhaps new curtains—

THÉRÈSE: No.

CAMILLE: It won't do?

THÉRÈSE: No, it's fine as it is. We're fine as we are.

MADAME: But, my dear—even I would admit that it needs a few touches—

THÉRÈSE: Of luxury? Why? What else do we need?

CAMILLE: We have each other.

MADAME: Is that what she means?

THÉRÈSE: What's narrow and cold and deep and smells like earth?

MADAME: Is this a riddle? What do you mean?

THÉRÈSE: I mean, we are fine as we are.

(2)

(THÉRÈSE *still sits.* MADAME *is knitting.*)

MADAME: When I was a girl, a summer day would stretch like taffy. On forever. One afternoon in the park would last a year. And now...when I have such a small part left of life...it's quite the other way round. I can't believe three years have passed since we moved into this place. Can you? Thérèse?

THÉRÈSE: What?

MADAME: Never mind. I forgot to tell you—I saw an old friend on the street today. Inspector Michaud. I knew him twenty-some years ago.... He plans to drop by after dinner.

THÉRÈSE: Ah.

MADAME: With his son and daughter-in-law, if we're lucky. And possibly one of Camille's fellow workers. I thought we could stay up just a bit late and play dominoes.

THÉRÈSE: Almost an orgy... What's narrow and cold and deep and smells like earth?

MADAME: Haven't you asked me this riddle before?

THÉRÈSE: Have I? (*Pause*) Are you happy?

MADAME: Well...

THÉRÈSE: Sad?

MADAME: Not sad.

THÉRÈSE: What are you, then?

MADAME: Content.

THÉRÈSE: Oh, god....

(3)

(Old MICHAUD, *his policeman son* OLIVIER, *and* OLIVIER's *wife* SUZANNE *and* CAMILLE's *dried up co-worker* GRIVET *have joined the* RAQUINS *for dominoes.)*

*(*THÉRÈSE *sits off to the side, watching the others play.)*

(No one speaks. Only the sound of dominoes clicking.)

MADAME: *(Offering a plate of candy)* Grapefruit peel?

(4)

*(*CAMILLE *is in bed.* THÉRÈSE *sits off in a chair, looking out the window.)*

(Suddenly, CAMILLE *cries out and sits up.)*

THÉRÈSE: Shhhh...

CAMILLE: I was sinking down into...something.
Cool and deep...

THÉRÈSE: You were dreaming.

CAMILLE: I couldn't breathe.

THÉRÈSE: It's alright. Go back to sleep.

CAMILLE: What are you doing?

THÉRÈSE: Trying to see the river.

CAMILLE: How can you see the river? There's just a brick wall.

THÉRÈSE: Sometimes, at night, when the traffic dies down, I think I can hear it.

CAMILLE: *(Straining to hear)* Now?

THÉRÈSE: No.

CAMILLE: Do you sit up often, alone, at night?

THÉRÈSE: Sometimes.

CAMILLE: You have secrets from me. I didn't know.

THÉRÈSE: Not many, Camille.

CAMILLE: What else?

THÉRÈSE: Nothing else. Sometimes at night I sit up and stare at the alley wall. You needn't alert the press.

CAMILLE: Come back to bed. I want to hold you.
I never dream when I hold you.

THÉRÈSE: I know.

(5)

(The domino players—old MICHAUD *and* GRIVET *and young* OLIVIER *and* SUZANNE—*are back. Again,* THÉRÈSE *sits off to the side and watches. No one speaks.)*

(Only the clack of the domino tiles)

MADAME: Perhaps you could open a window, Thérèse.

THÉRÈSE: Are you warm?

MADAME: I keep smelling an—odor. Like gas...

OLIVIER: It's probably me.

MADAME: No, certainly not...

(The clack of tiles)

OLIVIER: I had to go down to the morgue today.
The aroma clings....

(Silence falls.)

(The clack of tiles. Suddenly, SUZANNE gets up.)

SUZANNE: I seem to be having the slightest attack of the vapors. Excuse me.

(She runs off.)

MADAME: Thérèse—

OLIVIER: Don't bother. She won't be long.

(Silence falls. GRIVET puts down a domino. MICHAUD points out:)

MICHAUD: That's a *five*, Grivet. Put on your glasses.

(GRIVET takes back his tile, holds it close to his face. Then he searches for a piece he can play.)

GRIVET: What kind of aroma?

OLIVIER: You must have passed a dead dog, by the side of the road, on a very warm day....

GRIVET: As bad as that?

OLIVIER: Much worse.

(Silence. MADAME passes a tray.)

MADAME: Grapefruit peel?

(No takers—the game goes on.)

MICHAUD: When I was his age... *(He points to OLIVIER.)* a lowly gendarme...I wouldn't go down to the morgue at all. I simply wouldn't go. "You can have me up on charges," I said. "Or send me into the nearest den of thieves, unarmed— I will gladly go. But I have to draw a line."

(SUZANNE reenters, her forehead damp, and sits down.)

OLIVIER: All better?

(SUZANNE *nods.*)

GRIVET: I myself am glad I work in a humdrum office, with boring fellows, at work of no consequence whatsoever.

MICHAUD: That's a FIVE, Grivet!

(6)

(CAMILLE *and* THÉRÈSE *are getting ready for bed.*)

THÉRÈSE: What do you do all day?

CAMILLE: You know what I do.

THÉRÈSE: I don't. You go to the office.

CAMILLE: And then I come home.

THÉRÈSE: Are you happy?

CAMILLE: Not at the office.

THÉRÈSE: Where?

CAMILLE: At the zoo.

THÉRÈSE: What zoo?

CAMILLE: By the end of the day, by the end of one more endless column of figures, my mind is totally blank. It's nice. I let my feet decide my destination. The rest of me follows along.

THÉRÈSE: Your feet decide to go to the zoo.

CAMILLE: I don't know why. But I find myself outside a cage, four days out of five. And then I wake part-way up and I watch the bears. I can't believe how big they are. I can't believe how *there* they are.

THÉRÈSE: Do you feed them?

CAMILLE: No. I don't think I deserve to feed them.

THÉRÈSE: Don't say such things—

CAMILLE: But it's true! These beasts are forces, Thérèse. They roam about behind the bars, and I feel the sidewalk shuddering under my feet. I follow them step for step. On my side of the bars. When they stand on top of their toes, I stand. When they drop, I drop. When they maul each other, I hug myself as hard as I can. And then, when they slump into stupors, I find my way home.

(Pause)

THÉRÈSE: I might be a bear.

CAMILLE: But you aren't. Are you? Aren't you my little Thérèse?

(7)

(The domino players. THÉRÈSE sits off at the side. No-one speaks. The skeletal clack of tiles.)

(Then even the clacking fades. The room is completely still.)

THÉRÈSE: Has everyone died?

(She looks over. The silent players continue the domino-game, but in slow motion. THÉRÈSE stares at them, amazed.)

THÉRÈSE: Everyone has died, and their flesh is gone and I hear their bones.

(The clack of a tile)

THÉRÈSE: Falling apart: this clatter—rats wandering through a rib-cage...

(THÉRÈSE approaches the table now, where the domino-game goes on. No-one at the table responds to THÉRÈSE.)

THÉRÈSE: Did you know your bones are glowing?
I hold my hands to the light, but your glow is cold,
and my hands are shaking, because I am going out,
I am guttering out, I am almost nothing left but a bit
of burnt wick and a wisp of smoke. *(She makes the sound
of a candle being snuffed:)* "Ssssss..."

(The clack of a tile)

THÉRÈSE: What's narrow and cold and deep and smells
like earth? Don't you know? This isn't a riddle! This is
my life! This is the bed I have made and lie in every
night, in the dark I can hear you, stirring—"Clack!"
Coming closer, but my god—so slowly: "Clack!
CLACK!"

(THÉRÈSE beseeches the players, who cannot hear her.)

THÉRÈSE: Don't lurk about, then. Don't hold back.
Terrify me. Stop my heart. Don't leave me here,
entombed alive, to rot the way you rotted! Finish me!
Frighten me to death.

MADAME: *(A whisper)* Grapefruit peel?

THÉRÈSE: Grapefruit peel? GRAPEFRUIT PEEL?
(She laughs, a little hysterically.) I can't be frightened to
death. I'm already dead. And this is hell. *(She retreats
to her chair, still laughing.)*

(The domino-game fades in again, at its normal speed.)

GRIVET: Is that a five or an eight?

MICHAUD: It's a six.

MADAME: We might like to laugh too, Thérèse—

THÉRÈSE: It's nothing.

MADAME: Then why are you laughing?

THÉRÈSE: I heard of a road, outside of Paris, that runs
so long and so straight, without even the slightest bend,
that carriage drivers fall asleep at the traces....

MADAME: What happens after the drivers nod?

THÉRÈSE: The horses bolt, and the carriages overturn. The people inside are tossed about. Maybe they die.

MADAME: And you find this a source of amusement?

THÉRÈSE: No. *(But she starts to laugh again.)* I'm sorry... of course it's not funny at all....

(And she keeps on laughing, as MADAME *watches her, gravely.)*

(8)

*(*MADAME *and* THÉRÈSE *are in the shop,* THÉRÈSE *in her usual pose.)*

MADAME: I'm considering closing early, Thérèse. No one has come in.

THÉRÈSE: No one has come in for a week.

MADAME: We should put some new things in the window. Or dust the old ones.

THÉRÈSE: Or bury the old ones.

MADAME: I wonder if people peep in the window, and see you always sitting there, wearing that not-completely-inviting expression...

THÉRÈSE: In what way "not-completely-inviting"? No, tell me, Auntie—I don't have a clue as to how I appear, anymore. Do I frown?

MADAME: Well, it isn't exactly a frown—

THÉRÈSE: Do I sneer?

MADAME: No, it isn't a sneer....

THÉRÈSE: Do my lips curl up in a scornful smile?

MADAME: Your lips don't move.

THÉRÈSE: Am I darting daggers?

MADAME: No.

THÉRÈSE: Am I lost in some secret sorrow?

MADAME: I doubt it.

THÉRÈSE: Then what is my daunting expression?

MADAME: It's nothing. Like glancing down into an airshaft. Nothing at all.

(9)

(MADAME *and* THÉRÈSE *are in the shop.*)

MADAME: Why is Camille so late?

THÉRÈSE: He stops at the zoo.

MADAME: He doesn't.

THÉRÈSE: He watches the bears.

MADAME: He always *did* have a poetic soul.

(Just then CAMILLE *enters, pushing foward* LAURENT.*)*

CAMILLE: Ta-da!

MADAME: I beg your pardon?

CAMILLE: I said, "Ta-da!" I brought you a present! Imported at great expense from the drowsing countryside, and your long-lost past. You don't remember him?

MADAME: Do I ?

CAMILLE: Laurent! Remember Laurent? His father owned the high fields above the church.

MADAME: Little Laurent?

CAMILLE: The three of us used to play by the river—remember, Thérèse? *(To* MADAME*)* And he'd charm you into baking us little brown cookies—

MADAME: Laurent!

(She embraces him, and he gives her a crushing hug. THÉRÈSE *just stares.* MADAME *bursts into tears.)*

LAURENT: *(Handing* CAMILLE *a bottle)* You win.

CAMILLE: I bet Laurent a bottle of wine you'd start to bawl.

MADAME: So long ago...little Laurent...when I was a girl, a summer day—

CAMILLE: Now don't get started on summer days or we'll die of hunger right here in the shop. Can you feed this ox?

MADAME: Of course I can, there's stew, you can stay? My god in heaven—little Laurent...

CAMILLE: And guess where I found him? Sauntering out of the office, right behind me. He works for the company too, and we never suspected. That's what tiny cogs we are, in a vast machine...

MADAME: Let's all go up at once. Thérèse?

THÉRÈSE: *(In a trance)* Yes?

MADAME: Put out the light.

*(*MADAME *begins to lead the others out.)*

CAMILLE: You have to forgive my wife, Laurent— she's never seen a man before.

MADAME: She must have seen *you.*

CAMILLE: As I was saying...

*(*MADAME, CAMILLE, *and* LAURENT *exit.)*

*(*THÉRÈSE *sits, lost in thought.)*

(Then something makes her look up. She sniffs the air, then her hands.)

THÉRÈSE: What am I smelling?

(10)

(The domino players—old MICHAUD, GRIVET, MADAME, *young* OLIVIER, SUZANNE, *and* CAMILLE—*are now joined by* LAURENT.)

(As always, THÉRÈSE *sits off to one side.)*

GRIVET: Been back to the morgue, Olivier?

SUZANNE: *(Rushing in)* No. And if he *had*, he wouldn't discuss it. As per my request. That kind of talking makes me feel quite liverish, thank you so much.

GRIVET: A thousand pardons!

MICHAUD: Move, Grivet!

LAURENT: I've been to the morgue myself. A number of times.

CAMILLE: On a bet?

LAURENT: Not at all. With my artist-friends. In my long-ago *vie de boheme.*

MADAME: You didn't *paint*?

LAURENT: I'm afraid I did. While my skinflint papa paid my way, in the hugely mistaken impression that I was grooming myself for the law.

OLIVIER: Were you good?

LAURENT: No. But I liked the life.

(The men nudge each other and laugh.)

OLIVIER: By *life*, do you mean—

SUZANNE: He said "life". He meant "life". Let us leave
it at that.

GRIVET: But why the morgue?

LAURENT: We'd stand at the public window, with pad
in hand, and sketch the bodies.

OLIVIER: Didn't you have a supply of...warmer models?

LAURENT: I did—so I got down youth and beauty.
And then I moved on.

OLIVIER: Dead men on a table.

LAURENT: Children, crones, old drunks, and young,
a pregnant whore somebody fished out of the river—

CAMILLE: Naked?

LAURENT: The way she came into the world. Blue skin.
Wet hair. Great curve of belly. The very best thing I did,
my teachers said.

(Suddenly, SUZANNE gets up and runs from the table.)

MADAME: Thérèse?

THÉRÈSE: She won't be long.

CAMILLE: So why'd you hang up your brush?

LAURENT: My father came up to the garret one day.
And my model opened the door. As she was. My father
was so alarmed that he took a step backward and fell
down three flights of stairs.

MADAME: Was he hurt?

LAURENT: Not a bit. But *I* was. By the time he hit
bottom he'd cut me off. Without a cent.

MICHAUD: You weren't prepared to starve for your art?

LAURENT: Do I look like a man who would starve for
his art?

(The men laugh.)

(THÉRÈSE *gets up and moves away.*)

CAMILLE: Thérèse?

THÉRÈSE: I have to open a window.

(CAMILLE *gets up and crosses to* THÉRÈSE.
The domino players play.)

CAMILLE: What's wrong?

THÉRÈSE: Nothing. The air is close.

CAMILLE: Won't you sit at the table?

THÉRÈSE: My head is splitting.

CAMILLE: You never sit at the table, do you.
Laurent is certain you must dislike him.

THÉRÈSE: Why are his hands so large?

CAMILLE: Are they?

THÉRÈSE: Why is his neck so thick?

CAMILLE: Does it matter?

THÉRÈSE: Why doesn't he bathe?

CAMILLE: But he does.

THÉRÈSE: I can smell him from here.

CAMILLE: Look—if you *do* dislike him, he needn't come
round.

THÉRÈSE: I don't care. You like him.

CAMILLE: I like a good fire. He strikes me that way.
Someone I can warm my hands in front of.

GRIVET: (*At the table*) Ha! That's a THREE, Michaud!

(11)

(CAMILLE *poses;* LAURENT *paints.* THÉRÈSE *watches.*)

CAMILLE: Can I move?

LAURENT: No.

CAMILLE: I'm quite stiff.

LAURENT: Five minutes. The light is almost gone.

CAMILLE: I wish you would let us see it.

LAURENT: Bad luck.

MADAME: *(Off)* Thérèse?

*(*THÉRÈSE *doesn't move.)*

CAMILLE: I've tried, but I can't imagine it.

LAURENT: What?

CAMILLE: Standing there, with palette and brush in hand, while a woman takes off her clothes.

LAURENT: Can't you?

CAMILLE: I wouldn't know where to look.

LAURENT: There are dozens of places.

CAMILLE: My hand would shake.

MADAME: *(Off)* Thérèse!

CAMILLE: Should you see what she wants?

LAURENT: Don't move!

THÉRÈSE: A customer probably wandered into the shop. By mistake.

(Pause)

CAMILLE: I'd be hypnotized.

LAURENT: But the model is hypnotized too.

CAMILLE: She watches the brush? I do.

LAURENT: She watches my eyes.

CAMILLE: Do you look at her face?

LAURENT: I look at her body. Then I listen. I try to hear what the body is saying.

CAMILLE: "I have to go to the bathroom".

LAURENT: *(Laughing)* Maybe.

CAMILLE: "I have to be hungry. I have to ache. I have to shiver and sweat and prickle".

LAURENT: Well, yes...

CAMILLE: "I have to wear down. I have to stop".

LAURENT: The body says other things....

CAMILLE: I suppose. "Love me", you mean.

LAURENT: Or "save me".

THÉRÈSE: *(Low)* End me. *(Pause)* End me.

LAURENT: The first model I ever had was a beautiful redhead. *Natural* red, as I quickly discovered. With only the hitch that this wonderful creature was deaf as a brick. I couldn't call out if I wanted adjustments. I had to mold her pose like a sculptor. Part by part. One afternoon I wanted her legs to be just a bit wider. I tried to move her knees apart with my hands, but my touch was clumsy. Back and forth, and never right. And then, on a hunch, I touched the inside of her thigh with the tip of my brush. Where the skin is soft as cream. And warm. The lightest touch of camel's hair.

CAMILLE: Did she make the small move you were after?

LAURENT: She did.

CAMILLE: And what was her body saying?

LAURENT: "Brush me again".

(Pause)

THÉRÈSE: Did Madame call?

(MADAME enters.)

MADAME: Five minutes ago. Is it done?

LAURENT: It's a painting, Madame. Not a roast.

CAMILLE: Great art takes time—

MADAME: Just one small peek.

LAURENT: *(Shaking his head)* It can't be done.

MADAME: But I could be called to Heaven before you desist.

LAURENT: I doubt it, Madame. My guess would be that you'll see us all snug in our graves.

MADAME: *(In a huff)* I won't listen to talk like that. What a terrible thought! Thérèse? *(She exits.)*

(THÉRÈSE starts to follow her out.)

LAURENT: Don't move!

THÉRÈSE: But I'm in your light.

LAURENT: I've painted your shadow into the picture. Don't move.

(12)

(MADAME, THÉRÈSE, and CAMILLE are looking at the finished picture. LAURENT nervously waits for their reaction. MADAME moves closer to the canvas.)

LAURENT: The surface is wet.

MADAME: But it's done?

LAURENT: *(Nodding)* Don't touch it.

CAMILLE: I look...is "distinguished" the word?

MADAME: It's *a* word. You've painted him as if he were....

THÉRÈSE: *(Low, almost to herself)* Rotting.

MADAME: No, as if he were...

THÉRÈSE: Under water too long.

CAMILLE: As if I were...somehow...*serious*.

LAURENT: Thank you—I think.

MADAME: But it barely resembles you. It's so blue.
And so gray...

CAMILLE: It resembles my soul.

(MADAME *looks closer.*)

MADAME: Perhaps it does. You *were* always a serious
child. *(To* LAURENT*)* Were you after his soul?

LAURENT: It's an artist's duty, Madame.

MADAME: It grows on one.

LAURENT: So does mange.

MADAME: Don't belittle yourself. You've given us a
glimpse of...something eternal—

(Far off, the shop bell rings.)

MADAME: Not a customer *now*!

CAMILLE: Why don't you go down to the shop, maman.
And I'll run off to the store for a bottle of decent
champagne. *Two* bottles! And then we can come back
up to the parlor and celebrate Laurent's masterpiece.

MADAME: Agreed. But hurry—I can't get enough of this
picture! *(She exits.)*

CAMILLE: It really is an extraordinary thing.

(CAMILLE *runs off.*)

(THÉRÈSE *and* LAURENT *are left alone, together—
for the very first time.*)

(THÉRÈSE *is turned away from* LAURENT.)

LAURENT: Do you like it?

THÉRÈSE: You said you couldn't paint.

(She turns to face him. They stare at each other.)

(Pause)

LAURENT: Unbutton your blouse.

(She starts to do so.)

THÉRÈSE: We don't have time.

LAURENT: But maybe we do.

(He crosses to her and puts his hand inside her blouse.)

(She moans.)

LAURENT: Am I hurting you?

THÉRÈSE: Yes.

LAURENT: Don't moan.

THÉRÈSE: "Don't make a sound. Keep quiet..."
I can moan. I can scream! I'm a bear.

LAURENT: I know. So am I.

(He pulls her down onto the floor.)

Scene Three

(1)

(LAURENT sits back in an armless chair. THÉRÈSE straddles his legs and sits on his thighs, facing him. Her blouse is unbuttoned, her hair is down.)

(She unbuttons his shirt.)

MADAME: *(Off)* Thérèse?

THÉRÈSE: *(Yelling)* What is it?

MADAME: *(Off)* A customer!

THÉRÈSE: I'm coming!

(She bends to kiss LAURENT's *chest.)*

(2)

(THÉRÈSE *and* LAURENT *stand apart, staring at each other.)*

LAURENT: I'm afraid.

THÉRÈSE: Madame won't leave the shop undefended. As if a thief might want our goods. Camille's at work. You always use the back stairs, so no one can see you come or go.

LAURENT: Your marriage bed—

THÉRÈSE: —is the safest place we could possibly find. Who ever would look for us there?

LAURENT: I *am* afraid.

THÉRÈSE: And you wish I were.

(Pause)

LAURENT: I'm afraid of how lovely you are.

THÉRÈSE: Am I?

LAURENT: You weren't. Before.

THÉRÈSE: Do you know what makes a person ugly?

LAURENT: No.

THÉRÈSE: The fear of death.

LAURENT: Don't you think that you'll die now?

THÉRÈSE: Now I know I will. But it's like I'd been holding on to the edge of a cliff. For all of my life. And then I let go. I know I'll hit. I even know when. I can think about other things, for the very first time. I can notice the air. I can not be afraid.

LAURENT: While you fall.

THÉRÈSE: While I fly.

(3)

(LAURENT is fucking THÉRÈSE. He stands. Her legs are around his waist and he holds her ass.)

LAURENT: I tried not to come back.

THÉRÈSE: I know.

LAURENT: I tried!

(THÉRÈSE moans.)

MADAME: *(Off)* Thérèse?

LAURENT: For god's sake...

MADAME: *(Off)* Are you ill?

THÉRÈSE: *(Calling)* I have the most terrible migraine, Madame.

MADAME: *(Off)* Would you like some tea?

THÉRÈSE: Maybe later. Now I just want to....
(She whispers) ...screw.

LAURENT: Shut up!

MADAME: *(Off)* You want what?

THÉRÈSE: *(Calling)* To snooze!

(She turns back to LAURENT.)

LAURENT: You like to lie.

THÉRÈSE: I do. And I'm good. They made me good.
Listen: "*Thank* you for locking me up in a sickroom!
Thank you for letting me wed your bedridden son, with
his sour-pajama smell and his flesh like dough, and
thank you for burying me alive, in this shop, in this life,

in this body, thank you, thank you, thank you, thank you, thank you, thank you, thank you, thank you—"

(LAURENT *strangles a cry as he comes.*)

MADAME: *(Off)* Thérèse? Is the cat coughing up a fur ball?

(THÉRÈSE *starts to laugh, and laughs until she starts to cry.*)

LAURENT: *(A little out of breath)* Why are you crying?

THÉRÈSE: I'm not.

LAURENT: Tell me.

THÉRÈSE: You dug me up too late.

LAURENT: No. Just in time. Feel. *(He moves, still in her, comforting her.)* Just in time...

(4)

(THÉRÈSE *and* LAURENT *lie side by side on the floor. He touches her face.*)

THÉRÈSE: I hated you.

LAURENT: Why?

(She turns away. He climbs on top of her, kissing her hair and neck. She looks off.)

THÉRÈSE: Look at the cat...here, kitty kitty...sometimes I suspect that cat is the only honest soul in the house. And I think, one night, Camille will pick him up and the cat will say, "Did you know that Thérèse and Laurent are fond of lying on top of each other and making strange sounds?"

(He strokes her hair.)

LAURENT: You hated me?

THÉRÈSE: Before you ever touched me... I used to walk into a room, and I'd see you there, and you'd barely look up. But you knew—you could have me. If you wanted me. I'd want to sink my fingernails in your face. And I'd find myself moving around and around your chair...just to wander through your breath.

LAURENT: Do you hate me *now*?

THÉRÈSE: Yes.

LAURENT: Why?

THÉRÈSE: Because you can leave me.

(5)

(The domino players, around the table: GRIVET, MICHAUD, OLIVIER, SUZANNE, MADAME, CAMILLE, THÉRÈSE, *and* LAURENT)

(For the first time, THÉRÈSE *sits with the others.)*

(The clack of dominoes.)

GRIVET: Would you move?

*(*MICHAUD *puts down a tile.)*

MADAME: Grapefruit peel?

(She passes a tray around.)

THÉRÈSE: An hour ago, I was lying in there, behind that wall, on top of Laurent. One of my nipples was in his mouth. I would lower myself on his cock and then slowly rise up and then let myself down again, quickly, and slowly rise up....and our skin was hot and our mouths were dry and we had to cry out....and none of you heard. None of you knew. An hour ago. Behind that wall. I'm surprised you can't smell it, still. What we did. Right there.

(No one has heard her; no one reacts.)

CAMILLE: Thérèse?

THÉRÈSE: Hmm?

CAMILLE: Your move.

(6)

(LAURENT and CAMILLE are strolling, after work.)

LAURENT: If I had a wife like yours, Camille, I wouldn't dawdle so long after work.

CAMILLE: I wanted to show you something.

LAURENT: Here at the zoo?

(CAMILLE stares straight ahead, lost in thought.)

LAURENT: Camille? What are you doing?

CAMILLE: Watching the bears.

LAURENT: Why?

(Pause)

CAMILLE: Last week a little boy walked up to the bears, with a crust of bread he'd spread with honey, and gave it a heave, but his aim was bad. The honey-bread hit one bear on the back and stuck. And the bear could smell the honey but couldn't reach it. Look.

LAURENT: That one there, with the terrible wounds?

CAMILLE: The bear went wild. It mauled itself.

LAURENT: Why dwell on it? It's sad. Come on. Let's go.

(They start to walk off.)

CAMILLE: I don't know how to make Thérèse happy.

(LAURENT stops short.)

LAURENT: Isn't she happy?

CAMILLE: I don't even know how to tell.

(Pause)

LAURENT: Just love her, Camille.

CAMILLE: I do.

LAURENT: Just love her. See if she comes around.

(7)

(THÉRÈSE sits in a chair. LAURENT sits below her, resting his head on her lap. She strokes his hair.)

THÉRÈSE: I want to fall asleep in your arms.

LAURENT: I wish that could happen.

THÉRÈSE: I want to wake up with you there beside me. I want to touch your body while you sleep. Smell your warmth. Kiss you all over until you wake.

(There's a sudden knock at the door.)

MADAME: *(Off)* Thérèse?

(LAURENT is terrified. THÉRÈSE is excited.)

LAURENT: Oh, my god...

MADAME: *(Off)* I brought you some chamomile tea.

THÉRÈSE: Get under my skirts.

LAURENT: Do what?

THÉRÈSE: Get under!

(She lifts her skirts and drops them over LAURENT.)

LAURENT: *(Under the skirt)* Move your legs farther apart.

THÉRÈSE: No.

LAURENT: *(Under)* I can't breathe!

THÉRÈSE: I don't care!

(MADAME *enters.*)

MADAME: Were you dozing, my dear? I thought I heard you muttering.

THÉRÈSE: Maybe I was. I don't remember.

MADAME: Tea?

THÉRÈSE: Yes, please.

(*She takes the proffered cup.*)

MADAME: How is your head?

(*At that moment* LAURENT *begins to kiss her under her skirt.*)

(THÉRÈSE *gasps.*)

MADAME: Still agonizing?

THÉRÈSE: It comes and goes.

MADAME: Would you like me to rub your neck?

THÉRÈSE: I don't think—

(*She gasps again and writhes a bit as* LAURENT *kisses away.*)

MADAME: It used to help. When you were small.

(*Standing behind her,* MADAME *begins to massage* THÉRÈSE.)

(THÉRÈSE *is in an ecstasy of fear and pleasure.*)

MADAME: (*Singing*) "My brother was an officer,
he went away to sea;
he met someone, somewhere, somehow
and brought you home to me...."

(8)

(LAURENT and THÉRÈSE are sitting at the table, with MADAME.)

MADAME: Camille? What are you doing?

CAMILLE: *(Off)* Where is the tea?

MADAME: Right under your nose!

CAMILLE: *(Off)* What does it look like?

MADAME: *(Exiting)* It looks like tea!

(When she's gone, LAURENT stares at THÉRÈSE.)

LAURENT: Thérèse—

(But before he can speak, she leans across the table and kisses him fiercely.)

THÉRÈSE: *(Smiling)* What?

LAURENT: *(Whispered)* I can't come tomorrow. I got dressed down by my boss today. He said I'd been taking too much time off. No more long breaks for lunch. Or I get the sack.

(Pause)

THÉRÈSE: You can't come tomorrow?

(He nods.)

THÉRÈSE: Then when can you come?

(He shakes his head.)

(MADAME reenters and sits.)

MADAME: I've heard of people who couldn't boil water. I never suspected my son was one.
Shall I get the dominoes?

THÉRÈSE: No.

MADAME: Are you ill?

THÉRÈSE: I just don't want to play dominoes.

MADAME: What will we do?

(9)

(LAURENT *is pacing his tiny room like a beast in a cage.*)

(THÉRÈSE *appears.* LAURENT *sees her but looks away.
He stops.*)

LAURENT: I come back to this attic room, it's small,
I can barely move, the end of another day, without you,
and look at the dirty skylight—stars. Very far away.

(*He paces again. She joins him, pacing besides him.*)

LAURENT: Why did I think you were beautiful? Your
nose is long and your mouth is wide. And you make
this sound I hate, when you come, like somebody
gasping for air. And you have this smell I can't get out
of my clothes or off my hands. And you have this look
when I hold you... I don't love you at all.

(THÉRÈSE *and* LAURENT *keep pacing.* LAURENT *asks her,
without looking at her:*)

LAURENT: Are you there?

THÉRÈSE: No.

LAURENT: But I thought I heard your foot. On the stair.

(LAURENT *and* THÉRÈSE *both stop.* LAURENT *looks out,
as if trying to find someone in the dark.*)

LAURENT: Thérèse?

THÉRÈSE: It's only the old house settling. No one is there.

(THÉRÈSE *disappears.* LAURENT *senses her exit, without
seeing her go.*)

(*He starts pacing again, alone.*)

(10)

(LAURENT *is in the parlor.* THÉRÈSE *comes in.*)

THÉRÈSE: Don't go out tomorrow night.

LAURENT: Will you come? You have to come!

(*In answer she grabs his hand and kisses his palm, releasing him just as the domino players come in:* GRIVET, MICHAUD, OLIVIER, SUZANNE [*who's a little drunk*], MADAME, *and* CAMILLE.)

GRIVET: I don't believe you!

LAURENT: What don't you believe?

GRIVET: That a vast percentage of murderers get away.

LAURENT: According to who?

GRIVET: Inspector Michaud.

MICHAUD: It isn't something I'm proud of. Why would I lie?

SUZANNE: To get Grivet's old goat.

OLIVIER: But my father is merely expressing the terrible truth.

CAMILLE: I'm forced to take sides with my colleague here. Unless we all want to stay cowering under our beds, we have to assume the police are out there, doing their duty. By which I mean doing it well. Or else we'd never know if that man we bumped on the street was an unsuspected assassin.

MICHAUD: But it's very likely he was!

MADAME: No, certainly not!

MICHAUD: Let me give a for-instance, Madame Raquin.
Remember, back in Vernon, that baker we found
stuffed into his oven?

MADAME: Hacked to bits, I seem to recall.

MICHAUD: We never found his executioner, did we?

SUZANNE: Hacked to bits. How sad...

MICHAUD: For all we know, he's a neighbor of ours.
Grivet may see him tonight, when he's on his way
home.

GRIVET: If you wish to unnerve me, you've quite
succeeded. But still I insist, with a counter-example:
I heard of a servant who got locked up for stealing
the family silverware. And then, a year later, the family
cut a laburnum down and found the stolen goods in a
magpie's nest. The servant was freed, and justice
prevailed.

OLIVIER: I suppose they arrested the magpie, then.

SUZANNE: Hacked to bloody bits and baked in a pie.

MADAME: Is she all right?

OLIVIER: She had a Pernod.

CAMILLE: The police are impotent, then. And the sunlit
streets are full of bloodstained villains walking about
unafraid.

MICHAUD: Sad but true.

GRIVET: It's immoral!

MICHAUD: It's just the way things are.

(11)

(LAURENT *is pacing his room.*)

(THÉRÈSE *appears. She watches him. He senses her but won't look at her.*)

(*He keeps pacing alone, silently racing through the thoughts we heard him speaking before. At last he speaks out loud.*)

LAURENT: ...and you have this look, when I hold you....

THÉRÈSE: How do I look?

(LAURENT *stops pacing, startled at hearing a voice. He won't look at* THÉRÈSE, *still fearing she's a phantom.*)

LAURENT: And you have this smell...and you make this sound....

THÉRÈSE: (*More urgent*) But how do I look?

LAURENT: Like I could save you.

(THÉRÈSE *approaches him. He stares at her.*)

LAURENT: Are you there? (*He touches her face. The feel of her skin is shocking.*) Thérèse...

THÉRÈSE: Unbutton your shirt.

(*In a trance, he unbuttons his shirt. She starts to kiss his chest.*)

LAURENT: Oh, god. Thérèse...

THÉRÈSE: Don't talk.

LAURENT: I can't save you.

THÉRÈSE: I can't save *you.*

(12)

(LAURENT *and* THÉRÈSE *lie on the floor, in each other's arms.*)

(*A clock strikes ten.*)

THÉRÈSE: I have to go.

LAURENT: Don't go.

(She gets up, hurriedly putting herself together.)

THÉRÈSE: I have to go. I said I was tracking down an outstanding account.

LAURENT: Not very likely.

THÉRÈSE: It's all I could think of.

LAURENT: When will I see you again?

THÉRÈSE: Sometime.

(LAURENT gets up and grabs her arm.)

LAURENT: Not good enough. When?

THÉRÈSE: I don't know. I don't have many excuses for going out.

LAURENT: Then don't say "sometime." Say we won't meet again.

THÉRÈSE: No!... *(Furiously, she embraces him.)*

LAURENT: If only he'd—go away.

THÉRÈSE: People don't go away.

LAURENT: Sometimes they do...

(Pause)

THÉRÈSE: But it's dangerous. For the people they leave behind.

LAURENT: Not if the "going away" is an accident. Accidents happen. And then the people who went away never come back. That's all.

(Pause)

THÉRÈSE: I have to go.

(She starts to hurry away; he grabs her.)

LAURENT: Do I own you, Thérèse?

THÉRÈSE: Yes. Completely.

LAURENT: You own me.

(THÉRÈSE *hurries off.*)

(LAURENT *picks up the sheet on which she lay, and smells her scent.*)

(13)

(CAMILLE, LAURENT, *and* THÉRÈSE *are walking into a park outside the city. Autumn.*)

CAMILLE: Wasn't it summer an hour ago? And now the branches are almost bare. How did that happen?

THÉRÈSE: Listen...

CAMILLE: What?

THÉRÈSE: I hear water.

CAMILLE: Maybe it's leaves drifting down.

LAURENT: It's the river. Right beyond those trees.

(CAMILLE *is sitting down.*)

THÉRÈSE: Can we go there?

CAMILLE: Later. I thought we could rent a boat in a while and row out into the afternoon and watch the sun go down on the water.

THÉRÈSE: Tired?

CAMILLE: I couldn't have trudged another step. Just let me catch up with a couple of winks. Can I rest my poor head in your lap?

(THÉRÈSE *sits down.* CAMILLE *lies back, with his head on her skirt.*)

CAMILLE: Notice, Laurent—if *you* got married, you'd find yourself with a portable pillow.

LAURENT: Don't flaunt your good fortune, my friend.

CAMILLE: We must have walked twenty miles.

THÉRÈSE: Maybe two.

CAMILLE: *(Already drifting off)* I'm getting old. What an odd thought.

THÉRÈSE: Are you warm enough?

(In another moment, he's snoring.)

THÉRÈSE: Camille?

(CAMILLE is asleep. LAURENT sits down at THÉRÈSE's feet.)

(He starts to unbutton her shoe.)

THÉRÈSE: Don't!

LAURENT: I own you.

THÉRÈSE: Please...

LAURENT: I have to touch you.

(He pulls her shoe off, gently, taking care not to jostle CAMILLE.)

(Then he starts to kiss her foot.)

(She moans.)

(CAMILLE mutters in his sleep and then subsides.)

THÉRÈSE: Oh, god...

LAURENT: I know—

THÉRÈSE: No, you *don't* know—there! *(She points off:)* Clomping through the leaves...

MICHAUD: *(Off)* Is that Thérèse?

(THÉRÈSE stands and waves.)

SUZANNE: *(Off, to OLIVIER)* One boat ride. One. Was that too much to ask?

OLIVIER: *(Off, to* SUZANNE*)* With the sun going down. And the fog rolling in.

MICHAUD: *(Off)* And Laurent. Laurent!

(LAURENT *stands and forces a grin, waving.)*

GRIVET: *(Off)* And a sack of potatoes—

MICHAUD: *(Off, to* GRIVET*)* You blind old bat— that's Camille!

(THÉRÈSE *makes a shushing sign, with a finger to her lips, as* OLIVIER, SUZANNE, GRIVET, *and* MICHAUD *trudge in. They speak low to* THÉRÈSE.*)*

MICHAUD: *(Of* CAMILLE*)* Is he sick?

THÉRÈSE: He's napping.

GRIVET: On the damp ground? His mother would have a kitten. A litter.

THÉRÈSE: I won't tell, if *you* won't.

MICHAUD: *(To* THÉRÈSE, *of her shoeless condition)* What happened to your foot?

THÉRÈSE: A blister.

SUZANNE: *(To* OLIVIER*)* See? *(To* THÉRÈSE*)* I got one, too. *(To* OLIVIER*)* I told you this walk was too far.

OLIVIER: So we're going *back.*

SUZANNE: Without doing the single thing we came to do.

OLIVIER: If you want to rent a boat *now*, Suzanne, and row out into the fading light as icicles form along the oars, and the current you can't even see pulls you into the dark...be my guest. I'm heading home.

(OLIVIER *exits.)*

SUZANNE: Can I tell you something, Thérèse? (THÉRÈSE *leans in.)* All men are pigs.

(SUZANNE *exits.* GRIVET *and* MICHAUD *look out, as*
THÉRÈSE *and* LAURENT *keep hoping they too will go.*)

MICHAUD: We should have gone out on the water,
you know.

GRIVET: Is the boathouse closing?

MICHAUD: Next week. Until spring.

GRIVET: If only time would stop...

(*It seems to, for* LAURENT *and* THÉRÈSE, *as* MICHAUD *and*
GRIVET *regard the afternoon.*)

MICHAUD: ...but it never does. (*He points:*) See?
A wind's come up. And those leaves that might
have lasted another day are coming down.

OLIVIER: (*Off*) Father!

GRIVET: (*Looking off*) Your daughter-in-law is storming
off like she had quite a bee in her bonnet.

MICHAUD: Is she? (*He looks*) No—I believe it's an actual
bee. (*He shouts*) Don't swat it, Suzanne! They don't like
to be swatted... (*He hurries off.*)

GRIVET: Enjoy the afternoon.

(GRIVET *more sedately follows after* MICHAUD *and is gone.*)

(THÉRÈSE *puts her shoe back on. She can't look at* LAURENT.
CAMILLE *sleeps on.*)

THÉRÈSE: We should go.

LAURENT: Where?

THÉRÈSE: Back.

LAURENT: To what?

(THÉRÈSE *can't answer.* LAURENT *crosses to* CAMILLE.
Suddenly he raises his leg, as if to bring down his heel on
CAMILLE's *head.*)

(THÉRÈSE *gasps and turns away.*)

(Pause. Finally, LAURENT *eases his leg back down to the ground.)*

THÉRÈSE: *(Not looking around)* What are you doing?

LAURENT: Nothing.

(She looks around and sees that CAMILLE *is unharmed, asleep.)*

THÉRÈSE: The last time we could touch each other, Laurent, I stumbled home and to bed, and Camille was lying there, smelling the way he has always smelled, like a colicky child, and drool was trickling out of his lips, and I couldn't lie down beside him because.... I wanted to find a hammer. And hammer his sleeping face in.

*(*LAURENT *shakes his head.)*

LAURENT: It has to be an accident.

(Pause)

THÉRÈSE: Listen.

LAURENT: To what?

THÉRÈSE: The river.

(14)

(The river. LAURENT *is helping* CAMILLE *into a little boat.)*

LAURENT: Easy...

CAMILLE: I'd never make a sailor. Want to know why? I'm terrified of the water. That's why.

LAURENT: Don't stand in the boat, then. Sit.

*(*CAMILLE *sits at one end of the boat.)*

CAMILLE: If God had meant man to conquer the waves, He'd have fitted us out with pontoons instead of feet.

LAURENT: Don't be such a baby. Thérèse?

(He offers her his hand.)

THÉRÈSE: *(In a whisper)* What are you doing?

LAURENT: I'm going to throw him in.

(THÉRÈSE suddenly freezes. CAMILLE, looking out at the river, doesn't notice.)

CAMILLE: When we were small...remember, Thérèse? ...we'd play this game where we'd sit in a room, and the sun would go down, and you'd say, "Don't light a candle yet", and the light would fade, and we'd still be able to make things out in the room, a table, a lamp, a vase—but they'd lose their color, first, and then their edges...like the hills across the river...see? Where the tops of the trees are catching the final light? *(He watches.)* Gone...

LAURENT: *(Pulling)* Get in the boat, Thérèse.

(But still she resists.)

CAMILLE: And then, when it was completely dark...it'd feel like something else was with us. There in the room. I'd want to strike a match. You'd call me a baby. Remember?

LAURENT: *(To THÉRÈSE)* Come *on*.

CAMILLE: At least I'm not afraid of boats. Like *some* babies I could mention....

(THÉRÈSE stares right at CAMILLE.)

(And then she jumps in the boat.)

(She settles at the opposite end from CAMILLE.)

(LAURENT sits down in the middle and starts to row.)

CAMILLE: Is there anything as depressingly calm as an autumn afternoon?

*(*LAURENT *rows on.)*
(Lights fade out.)

END OF ACT ONE

ACT TWO

Scene One

(1)

(MADAME *is asleep at the table between* OLIVIER *and* SUZANNE, *who are playing dominoes, flanked by* MICHAUD *and* GRIVET. THÉRÈSE *and* LAURENT *sit apart from each other and farther off, watching.* THÉRÈSE *and* MADAME *are in mourning dress.)*

(MADAME *begins to snore.)*

SUZANNE: *(A loud whisper)* Is she sleeping?

THÉRÈSE: *(Whispered)* Yes.

SUZANNE: Perhaps we should leave—

(Using this as his cue, LAURENT *gets up.)*

THÉRÈSE: No, no...

(She gives LAURENT *a long look. He sits back down.)*

OLIVIER: We weren't at all sure we should come.

SUZANNE: But it's over a year. And we've missed your soirees.

THÉRÈSE: She's missed them too. Please stay.

(Satisfied, OLIVIER *plays a tile. The "clack" is loud.)*

GRIVET: Do you still go down to the morgue?

LAURENT: When they bring one in from the river.
He doesn't appear.

MADAME: *(Sitting up)* I see him breaking the surface,
sometimes.

LAURENT: We thought you were sleeping.

MADAME: Swelling. Bursting—

SUZANNE: Madame, I beg you—

MADAME: —apart. And other times, I see the boat
tipping, I see him falling, and then I see him swimming
away. Broad, powerful strokes. Flopping up onto the
bank, exhausted and happy...and I wonder: Why
couldn't it be that way? Why couldn't it be....

(No one answers.)

(MADAME nods off again and begins to snore.)

(MICHAUD plays a tile.)

GRIVET: Quiet!

MICHAUD: *(To* LAURENT*)* The men at my club want to
give you a dinner.

LAURENT: Whatever for?

MICHAUD: For your selfless efforts in trying to save him.

GRIVET: That party at the boathouse saw you diving
again and again—

LAURENT: Tell them no. No dinner. No medals. I lost
him. Let me sink out of sight too.

(SUZANNE puts down a tile.)

OLIVIER: Are you certain? *(To his wife) Count* the *dots,*
Suzanne.

SUZANNE: *(Pointing at the sleeping* MADAME*)* Shhhh!

OLIVIER: Shhhh!

(Silence falls, except for the clack of tiles, as SUZANNE *and* OLIVIER *play.)*

*(*THÉRÈSE *and* LAURENT, *the table between them, inspect each other.)*

THÉRÈSE: Why did we kill him?

LAURENT: To be together.

*(*THÉRÈSE *begins to laugh at this thought.* LAURENT *frowns at her. The other domino players regard her solicitously.* MADAME *wakes up.)*

MADAME: Thérèse? Did you say something?

THÉRÈSE: No, Madame. You must have been dreaming.

MADAME: Did I cry out?

THÉRÈSE: No.

MADAME: Then I wasn't dreaming.

(She sinks back into a doze again. The domino play resumes.)

LAURENT: Let me come to your room tonight.

THÉRÈSE: No! We have to wait—

LAURENT: It's been a year! *(Pause)* You look older.

THÉRÈSE: You're eating more.

LAURENT: Do you miss me?

THÉRÈSE: I lie in that great big empty bed completely alone, and I feel like a little girl again, the bed is a ship and the sheets are sails and my body is drifting away, it's nice...except....

LAURENT: What?

THÉRÈSE: Sometimes it gets dark and a wind comes up, and the water chops and the bed bumps up against something. Under the surface.

LAURENT: Can I touch you? *(He looks at her.)* I can't
touch you.

THÉRÈSE: Have you taken a mistress?

LAURENT: No.

THÉRÈSE: What does she look like?

LAURENT: Nothing. Smoke. You. I came back to my
room last week, and she was gone.

THÉRÈSE: Why?

LAURENT: I'd be dreaming, holding her tight, and I'd
whisper your name in her ear. She'd be sulky for hours.

THÉRÈSE: What do you dream?

LAURENT: That I'm walking down the dark street, in my
night shirt only, into your horrible alley and up the
back stair to your door, and I knock—

THÉRÈSE: And I open?

LAURENT: All in white in your nightdress, yes.
You open. Only...

THÉRÈSE: What?

LAURENT: The last few nights it hasn't been you who
opens.

THÉRÈSE: Who?

LAURENT: I don't remember. I wake up screaming.

(Pause)

THÉRÈSE: Why did you take a mistress?

LAURENT: Why were you happy alone in your little
girl's bed?

THÉRÈSE: I'm afraid of you.

LAURENT: I'm afraid of you.

(MADAME wakes with a cry.)

(The domino players stand.)

SUZANNE: We've worn you down—

MADAME: And I thank you for that. You must promise to come back soon.

OLIVIER: If you promise to bury those morbid thoughts. You mustn't imagine Camille in bits and pieces, Madame.

MADAME: How should I imagine him?

OLIVIER: Gone.

(The domino players exit. MADAME watches them go.)

MADAME: Were they always so selfish?

THÉRÈSE: Are they now?

MADAME: They find my grief an inconvenience.

LAURENT: Perhaps they don't want you to suffer.

MADAME: I doubt it. It's decent of you to imagine it, though. You have a kind heart.

LAURENT: Don't say it, Madame.

MADAME: But you do. Don't you think so, Thérèse?

THÉRÈSE: How could I not?

MADAME: You light our fires, you sweep our steps, you empty the trash—

LAURENT: It's nothing, Madame.

MADAME: No, it isn't nothing. It's comfort, Laurent. And you've given it gladly—

LAURENT: I should have come by more often.

MADAME: You came enough.

(She kisses LAURENT and starts to exit.)

MADAME: Close up the shop as you leave?

LAURENT: Of course.

(MADAME *exits*)

(THÉRÈSE *and* LAURENT *stare at each other.*)

LAURENT: Why did we kill him?

THÉRÈSE: To be together.

LAURENT: I want you, Thérèse.

THÉRÈSE: Oh, god...

LAURENT: I'm afraid without you.

THÉRÈSE: I am, too.

(Pause)

LAURENT: We have to make them want a wedding.

THÉRÈSE: How?

LAURENT: Can you grieve a little more?

(THÉRÈSE *nods, understanding his plan.*)

(2)

(The following day. THÉRÈSE—*alone*—*is seated, lying in wait for* MADAME.*)*

MADAME: (Off) Thérèse! Have you made any tea?

(To practice grieving, THÉRÈSE *dishevels her hair and forces some tears, sobbing audibly.)*

MADAME: *(Off)* Thérèse! THÉRÈSE! What is that sound? *(She hurries in, alarmed.)* Are you crying?

THÉRÈSE: Am I?

(THÉRÈSE *feels the tears on her cheeks, feigning surprise.* MADAME *is even more afraid.)*

MADAME: If you left me, Thérèse...

THÉRÈSE: I'm not planning a trip.

MADAME: But if you departed...

THÉRÈSE: For where?

MADAME: *(Cornered)* I meant, if you died...

THÉRÈSE: *(Considering)* Of a broken heart...

MADAME: People do. I'd be all alone.

(Horrified at the thought of being abandoned, MADAME *comforts* THÉRÈSE).

(3)

*(*LAURENT *is pacing his tiny room, holding a candle. He looks out into the dark.)*

LAURENT: Camille?

(4)

*(*MICHAUD, GRIVET, OLIVIER, *and* SUZANNE *play dominoes with* MADAME.*)*

MICHAUD: How sick is Thérèse?

MADAME: I beg your pardon! Don't even suggest it—she's perfectly well—

MICHAUD: She's white as a slab of marble, Madame. Her eyes are empty. Her skin is dull. And either she's sick as a dog....

GRIVET: Or what?

MICHAUD: Or she's sicker of lying alone in an empty bed.

OLIVIER: Father!

MICHAUD: Well, wouldn't you be?

(SUZANNE *covers her face with her hands.*)

MICHAUD: Excuse my bluntness, Madame—

MADAME: Not at all. I only wonder if anyone even remembers—

GRIVET: What?

MADAME: That I had a son. Who died. Who died again, when you said that his wife should go on with her life.

SUZANNE: But shouldn't Thérèse go on?

MADAME: Yes. I want her to live. I don't want to be left alone...but who could she marry?

(*At that moment* THÉRÈSE *and* LAURENT *walk on, across the room, engaged in quiet conversation. The domino players eye the couple.*)

MICHAUD: Who else but Laurent?

MADAME: Laurent. Kind-hearted Laurent...

(*Out of earshot of the domino players,* THÉRÈSE *and* LAURENT *begin to speak.*)

THÉRÈSE: Are you afraid? When you go to the morgue?

LAURENT: They run water over the corpses. To drown the stench. I was watching a body that lay in the path of one of those jets. The water was boring a hole in the face. And then all of a sudden the lips and nose came away and I saw the white teeth and the bones of the skull. Like the corpse was grinning.

THÉRÈSE: You thought it was him.

LAURENT: It *was* him. One of the fingers still had enough flesh to hold a ring.

THÉRÈSE: The ring I gave him?

LAURENT: Yes.

(THÉRÈSE *is stunned. She glances at* MADAME, *who waves.*)

THÉRÈSE: Why haven't you told her?

LAURENT: I thought I would let her hope, one final
night.

THÉRÈSE: And me?

LAURENT: Let's marry, Thérèse. They want us to. Look.

(*They glance at the domino players, who grin and wave.*)

THÉRÈSE: Last night I dreamed he was there at my door.

LAURENT: I dreamed he was climbing my stair. But he
wasn't, Thérèse. He was cold on a slab in the morgue.

THÉRÈSE: Don't!

LAURENT: And tomorrow we bury his bones.
And the past. And go on.

(*She stares at him. The domino players, thinking that*
THÉRÈSE *and* LAURENT *are about to kiss, burst into*
applause.)

(MADAME *comes down from the table to join the couple.*)

MADAME: Make her happy, Laurent, only that.
And my son will look down from his cloud and smile.

MICHAUD: (*Calling out from the table*) And kiss her,
for heaven's sake. Before we all start sobbing.

(THÉRÈSE *and* LAURENT *finally, chastely kiss and then jerk*
apart—as if the kiss had burned.)

(5)

(LAURENT *and* THÉRÈSE *are alone at last, preparing for*
bed—their wedding night.)

(LAURENT *unbuttons his shirt;* THÉRÈSE *steps out of her dress and stands in her bodice and petticoat, shoulders bare, staring out the window.*)

LAURENT: What are you doing?

THÉRÈSE: Watching the wall.

LAURENT: Why? (*He crosses to her and looks out.*)
It's just a brick wall.

THÉRÈSE: That's why. I like it just being a wall.

(*He kisses her shoulder. She pulls away and sits on a bench by the hearth.*)

LAURENT: Madame has outdone herself with our room...a fire and flowers and fresh white sheets...

THÉRÈSE: Listen...

LAURENT: What?

THÉRÈSE: The logs are wet. You can hear the hiss of the steam escaping...

(LAURENT *sits down on the other end of the bench.*)

LAURENT: Can I touch you? (*He looks at her.*)
I can't touch you.

THÉRÈSE: The scar on your neck...

LAURENT: (*Touching it nervously*) What about it?

THÉRÈSE: It turns bright red when you blush.

LAURENT: Does it?

THÉRÈSE: (*As she reaches to touch it*) How did you get it?

LAURENT: (*Too sudden, flinching away*) Don't!...

THÉRÈSE: I can't touch you? (*They stare at each other.*)
Your flesh is dead. And so is mine.

LAURENT: No! Our flesh is so alive that it frightens us.
Now that we've dreamed this night so long. And the

dream's come true. You wanted to fall asleep in my arms. You wanted to wake with me warm beside you. You wanted to kiss me all over until I stirred.

THÉRÈSE: Did I?

(LAURENT *and* THÉRÈSE *move closer together along the bench, until they are almost touching.*)

LAURENT: And now we can.

THÉRÈSE: But we have to sleep first. Before we wake.

LAURENT: And now we can. We can fuck and sleep and wake in each other's arms. Now that Camille is gone—

(THÉRÈSE *rears back in horror.*)

THÉRÈSE: No. Oh no. Oh, my god. My god. Why did you say his name?

LAURENT: *You* say it.

THÉRÈSE: I can't...

LAURENT: *(Firm but not harsh) Say* it, Thérèse.

THÉRÈSE: "Camille..."

(*They wait a moment, suspended.*)

LAURENT: See? What happens?

THÉRÈSE: Nothing...

LAURENT: Because? (THÉRÈSE *can't answer.*)

LAURENT: Because he's *dead*. Camille. Camille! CAMILLE!

(*Pause. The lovers try to recover their bearings.*)

LAURENT: Where do you think she got roses this time of year?

THÉRÈSE: She goes to a greenhouse.

LAURENT: Oh.

(Pause)

THÉRÈSE: *(To see what happens)* Camille. Camille!
CAMILLE!

LAURENT: See? He won't come. Keep calling. He won't.

THÉRÈSE: CAMILLE!

LAURENT: Do you *want* him to come?

THÉRÈSE: How badly did he die?

(LAURENT *doesn't know how to answer.*)

(Pause)

LAURENT: Didn't you see?

THÉRÈSE: I closed my eyes.

LAURENT: When?

THÉRÈSE: You had pulled him up out of his seat.
He thought you were kidding. "Don't tickle," he said.
"You'll make me fall in."

LAURENT: Then he looked in my face. He must have
seen something. He seemed surprised. He started to
shout—

THÉRÈSE: That's when I closed my eyes. *(Pause)*
Did he try to hold on—to the side of the boat?

LAURENT: I was faster than that. I was gentle, Thérèse.

THÉRÈSE: Show me how.

(*Very gingerly,* LAURENT *sweeps up* THÉRÈSE *and holds her
in his arms.*)

THÉRÈSE: He cried out?

LAURENT: No.

THÉRÈSE: I heard him. I closed my eyes—I couldn't
close my ears.

LAURENT: He called your name.

THÉRÈSE: Let me hear.

LAURENT: Like he was saying goodbye... *(Softly)*
Thérèse! Thérèse!

THÉRÈSE: And then?

LAURENT: And then I lowered him into the water.

THÉRÈSE: He didn't fight?

LAURENT: He was quiet. Like it was bath time.

THÉRÈSE: Show me?

(LAURENT very gently lowers her to the floor. He stays near her, wanting to touch her more, but afraid.)

LAURENT: And then he was gone. That's all.

THÉRÈSE: Except, when he started to disappear—did he look like that? *(She points at the unseen portrait of* CAMILLE.*)* Like your terrible picture?

LAURENT: It *is* terrible. Isn't it?

(THÉRÈSE starts to laugh. LAURENT joins in. With the tension eased for just a moment, LAURENT helps THÉRÈSE to her feet.)

(Holding hands, they approach the painting, like children egging each other on to enter a haunted house.)

LAURENT: What do you hate about it the most?

THÉRÈSE: The way the eyes float out of the sockets.

LAURENT: But didn't they? When he was alive?

THÉRÈSE: *(Becoming more uneasy)* I can't remember. What he looked like.

LAURENT: Good.

THÉRÈSE: Is it?

LAURENT: Why do you *want* to remember?

THÉRÈSE: So I can keep hating him. If I stopped...

LAURENT: *(Afraid of the answer)* What?

(THÉRÈSE, *unwilling to answer, touches the scar on her lover's neck.)*

LAURENT: The wound is so raw.

LAURENT: You could heal it. Kiss it. Please.

THÉRÈSE: How did you get it?

(LAURENT *doesn't respond.)*

THÉRÈSE: Did he do it?

LAURENT: It's nothing. Kiss me.

THÉRÈSE: Not there!

LAURENT: Please.

THÉRÈSE: There's blood.... *(She stares at him.)*

(Suddenly he takes her head in his hands and forces her face to his wound.)

(She struggles, but only a moment, and then goes limp, as he presses her lips to his scar.)

(When he lets her go, she jerks away and wipes her mouth as hard as she can.)

(Then she spits on the floor.)

(Pause)

LAURENT: I'm sorry. I thought your lips would be cool....

THÉRÈSE: No.

LAURENT: I thought the pain might stop. But it only got worse, and I—

(He stops because THÉRÈSE isn't paying attention. She's staring at the painting.)

THÉRÈSE: Look. He moved.

LAURENT: What?

THÉRÈSE: He *moved*. His face. His eyes, and the curl of his lip...

LAURENT: Isn't that how I painted him?

THÉRÈSE: I don't remember! —what he looked like! Do you?

LAURENT: *Is* he moving?

THÉRÈSE: Take it down.

LAURENT: *(Very uneasy)* In the morning.

THÉRÈSE: Take it down now.

(LAURENT doesn't move.)

THÉRÈSE: He *didn't* go gently, did he?

LAURENT: No. He struggled.

THÉRÈSE: Show me.

(LAURENT picks up THÉRÈSE again.)

LAURENT: You show *me*. I had to pry his fingers loose. He fought.

(THÉRÈSE starts to struggle in LAURENT's arms. LAURENT again lowers her to the stage. THÉRÈSE tries to bite LAURENT on the neck.)

LAURENT: What are you doing?

THÉRÈSE: He bit you.

LAURENT: *(Holding her off)* Yes!....

(When LAURENT has wrestled her onto the floor, he pushes her down, as if holding him underwater.)

THÉRÈSE: YOU HELD HIM UNDERWATER?

LAURENT: Didn't you hear him thrashing? Trying to find the air? He screamed.

(THÉRÈSE tries to break the surface of the "water".)

THÉRÈSE: "Thérèse! *Thérèse!*"

(LAURENT *releases her.*)

LAURENT: He wanted to touch you. One last time.

THÉRÈSE: "THÉRÈSE!"

(THÉRÈSE *lies on the floor where she's "drowned."*
LAURENT *tries to comfort her.*)

LAURENT: Shh....shhh...

THÉRÈSE: (*Not looking up, of* CAMILLE's *painting.*)
Is he watching?

(LAURENT *looks up at the painting and lies.*)

LAURENT: No.

THÉRÈSE: But *you* are.

LAURENT: You look like a little girl, in this light.

THÉRÈSE: I was never a little girl.

(*Pause*)

LAURENT: Do you know what this is? I'd almost
forgotten.

THÉRÈSE: What?

LAURENT: Our wedding night.

Scene Two

(1)

(THÉRÈSE *and* LAURENT *have stayed awake all night,
sitting up, on the bench.*)

THÉRÈSE: Did you sleep?

LAURENT: (*Eyes shut*) No.

THÉRÈSE: Open your eyes.

LAURENT: Why?

THÉRÈSE: First light.

(LAURENT *looks around at the portrait.*)

LAURENT: It's just a picture.

THÉRÈSE: Of course it is.

LAURENT: A terrible picture. What's wrong with us?
We were acting like children.

THÉRÈSE: Maybe tonight will be better.

LAURENT: No "maybe" about it. It *has* to be better.
I didn't get married to sit up quaking all night.

THÉRÈSE: Why *did* you get married?

(*Pause*)

LAURENT: Just try to be brighter tonight. Don't chill my
blood.

THÉRÈSE: All right. I'll try.

(2)

(*Late at night.* THÉRÈSE *and* LAURENT *are sitting clothed on
the end of the bed, terrified—unable to go to sleep.*)

LAURENT: Move closer. A little closer. An inch.

THÉRÈSE: I can't.

LAURENT: Why not?

THÉRÈSE: *You* move closer.

LAURENT: There isn't room. You know there isn't room.

(*Pause. They look at the space between them.*)

THÉRÈSE: I sleep in the shop. At the counter. What do
you do?

LAURENT: I nod off at my desk. Completely out. I even snore. They've reprimanded me twice in the last three days. *(Pause)* This has to stop. Why did we kill him?

THÉRÈSE: To be together.

LAURENT: Why did we wait so long to marry?

THÉRÈSE: So no one would know.

LAURENT: Why did we marry?

THÉRÈSE: To save ourselves. From him.

(Pause)

LAURENT: Give me a kiss.

THÉRÈSE: All right.

(They lean across an empty space to kiss.)

(Below and between them, the bedsheets start to writhe, as if something were under them.)

(Then the thing on the bed sits up between LAURENT *and* THÉRÈSE.*)*

*(*THÉRÈSE *pulls away from* LAURENT, *in horror. She seems to sense—without seeing—the thing beneath the sheet.)*

LAURENT: What's wrong? Why are you shaking? Who do you think is here?

(In a trance, THÉRÈSE *begins to pull off the sheet—revealing the drowned and rotting corpse of* CAMILLE.*)*

*(*LAURENT *can't quite see the corpse yet.)*

LAURENT: *Who?*

THÉRÈSE: Camille...

LAURENT: And what is he doing—thumbing his rotting nose?

THÉRÈSE: Just sitting.

LAURENT: Maybe we ought to go out to the graveyard.
Dig him up. Open his coffin. Show you where all that's
left of him's resting....

THÉRÈSE: Laurent, he is sitting right here!

LAURENT: Let him watch us, then. If it makes him glad.

(He stands and pulls THÉRÈSE to her feet.)

*(He wants to embrace her. But now he begins to sense
CAMILLE.)*

LAURENT: Thérèse...

THÉRÈSE: What?

LAURENT: I can smell the river.

THÉRÈSE: I know.

LAURENT: Is he here?

THÉRÈSE: Yes.

*(They break apart. THÉRÈSE and LAURENT move away from
the corpse.)*

THÉRÈSE: Your wound is open.

LAURENT: Is it? *(She approaches him.)*

THÉRÈSE: If only that wound would heal,
I think we could sleep....

LAURENT: Don't touch it.

THÉRÈSE: Let me just kiss it.

LAURENT: No.

THÉRÈSE: Let me burn it closed...

(In agony, he lets her kiss the scar on his neck.)

(She pulls away.)

THÉRÈSE: It's on fire.

LAURENT: I know. And your touch is like salt.

(Pause)

(They stare at one another, ignoring CAMILLE.*)*

(And then, in tender desperation, they try to kiss each other, gently.)

(Their lips are about to touch, when CAMILLE *sticks out his hand between them.)*

(They kiss either side of his hand.)

THÉRÈSE: I can't feel you.

LAURENT: I can't feel you.

(3)

*(*MADAME *sits up at the table between* THÉRÈSE *and* LAURENT, *drinking a cup of tea.)*

MADAME: When I was a girl, a summer day...

(She loses her train of thought. Pause.)

THÉRÈSE: Tell us about a summer day.

MADAME: I babble on and on and on.

LAURENT: We enjoy it, Madame.

THÉRÈSE: It's soothing.

MADAME: Is it? On and on and on and on...

THÉRÈSE: If we didn't have you...

LAURENT: It'd just be the two of us.

THÉRÈSE: All alone in the gloom.

MADAME: Would that be so bad?

*(*THÉRÈSE *and* LAURENT *exchange a glance.)*

MADAME: I thought you might *like* to be alone...

THÉRÈSE: That's nonsense, Auntie. You can't ever leave us. Promise.

MADAME: I wish I could... When I was a girl, a day spun out like...sugar. Spun...what? What spun?

THÉRÈSE: *(Prompting)* A day spun out like sugar...

MADAME: Melting...We thought the cow-flops were stepping-stones, and Amalie stepped on one and screamed and jumped to the next and screamed again...And I laughed so hard that I—

(MADAME freezes.)

(Long pause)

THÉRÈSE: That you what?

(MADAME drops the cup from her hand.)

(THÉRÈSE anxiously kneels in front of her.)

THÉRÈSE: Auntie?

LAURENT: What's happened?

THÉRÈSE: I think she's had a stroke.

LAURENT: Oh, god...

THÉRÈSE: We're all alone.

(4)

(THÉRÈSE sits next to MADAME, who's completely immobile. LAURENT looks anxiously on.)

THÉRÈSE: The doctor says you should try to move. The tiniest bit. Can you move your hand? Or even your finger?...No?

(In the silence, the tick of a clock is very loud.)

LAURENT: Say something, Madame. You have to keep talking. Babble. Chitter. Moan...

(The clock ticks on.)

THÉRÈSE: She can hear our thoughts.

LAURENT: I don't think so, Thérèse.

THÉRÈSE: In this silence? Don't you imagine?...

LAURENT: *(To* MADAME*)* Can you?

(Tick-tock, tick-tock)

MADAME: How long does it take to drown?

THÉRÈSE: We can't hear *hers*.

LAURENT: Maybe she doesn't have thoughts, anymore. Maybe she just drifts down...

MADAME: I do. How long does it take?

(The silence is deeper. Tick-tock.)

MADAME: And it isn't so horrible. Drifting down. The light is darker. Sound is softer. I think, I will turn, in the murk—and see someone I know. Someone I love...

(The clock ticks on.)

LAURENT: Thérèse.

THÉRÈSE: What?

LAURENT: Stop the ticking.

THÉRÈSE: No. That clock is the only sound that drowns you out.

LAURENT: I'm not saying a word.

THÉRÈSE: But you are. I can hear you. She must, too.

LAURENT: What am I saying?

THÉRÈSE: Exactly what *I* am saying, Laurent— *(In time with the ticking clock)* The shore, the boat, the afternoon, the sun gone down, the fog, the damp, the water dripping off the oars—

LAURENT: Will you *shut up?*

(Tick-tock)

MADAME: Don't fight, my children. Please. Let me drift to the end. Protected by you.

(The clock ticks on.)

(In silence, THÉRÈSE *and* LAURENT *try not to think. But their minds race on, in time to the ticking clock.)*

LAURENT: The sun gone down, the fog, the cold,

THÉRÈSE: —the water dripping off the oars,

LAURENT: —the fog is lifting off the water,

THÉRÈSE: —other boats are coming in,

LAURENT: —we're all alone.

(Tick-tock)

THÉRÈSE: The shore is gone, the boat is dark,

LAURENT: —I ship the oars, the water drips,

THÉRÈSE: —He sees your face.

(Tick-tock)

LAURENT: He sees my face.

THÉRÈSE: He starts to shout.

LAURENT: I grab his throat.

MADAME: Thérèse!

(Tock)

THÉRÈSE: He starts to shout: "Thérèse!"

(Tock)

LAURENT: I hold him up, he bites my neck, I heave him in, he surfaces,

THÉRÈSE: —he cries my name—

MADAME: Thérèse...

(Tock)

LAURENT: And then he's gone.

THÉRÈSE: He's gone.

(Tock)

MADAME: And then he's gone.

(THÉRÈSE notices the tears of MADAME.)

THÉRÈSE: My god. She heard us. Look: tears.

LAURENT: She couldn't have heard our thoughts—

THÉRÈSE: They weren't thoughts. We were speaking aloud. We didn't even know we were speaking aloud....

MADAME: My children have killed my child. My children have killed my child. My children have killed my child.

(5)

(MADAME at the table, immobile. THÉRÈSE and LAURENT are sitting on either side; THÉRÈSE is embroidering.)

THÉRÈSE: When did you quit your job? *(He doesn't respond.)* I went to your office today. They said you were gone.

(Pause)

LAURENT: Don't follow me, Thérèse.

THÉRÈSE: Why not?

LAURENT: I'll follow you.

THÉRÈSE: I have to get tired. I take long walks.

LAURENT: Beer you spill in the sun has a different smell.

THÉRÈSE: Does it?

LAURENT: From beer you spill in the dark. *(Pause)*
You smell like afternoon beer and smoke.

THÉRÈSE: I meet friends.

LAURENT: New friends.

THÉRÈSE: They'd have to be new. *(Pause)*
You smell like paint and turpentine.

LAURENT: I've rented a studio.

THÉRÈSE: Have you? How very sad.

LAURENT: Pour me a glass of water.

THÉRÈSE: Pour it yourself.

*(LAURENT pours out a glass from a dusty carafe.
He takes a sip.)*

LAURENT: It's warm.

THÉRÈSE: I couldn't get ice.

LAURENT: And it tastes like silt.

THÉRÈSE: Then leave it be.

LAURENT: In fact, it tastes like river water.

THÉRÈSE: Don't...

LAURENT: Do you meet your friends by the river?

THÉRÈSE: Please...

LAURENT: Do you lay yourself down by the waters and
weep? Do you lift your skirts and then trail your hand?
Do you squeeze the mud between your fingers and
wonder if some of his rot is there? Do you bring him
back to drink?

(THÉRÈSE backs away from the table, stunned.)

THÉRÈSE: YOU killed him.

LAURENT: Go on.

THÉRÈSE: *I* didn't kill him.

LAURENT: I thought that's what you thought. Funny.

(He grabs her, controlled but furious.)

LAURENT: Remember stepping down into the boat?

THÉRÈSE: No.

(He shakes her.)

LAURENT: Remember? DON'T YOU REMEMBER?

THÉRÈSE: Yes.

LAURENT: What did you whisper? *(She doesn't respond. He shakes her.)* What did you whisper?

THÉRÈSE: "What are you going to do?"

LAURENT: And what did I answer?

THÉRÈSE: You said you were going to throw him in.

LAURENT: And what did you do? *(She doesn't respond. He doesn't shake her. He only looks in her eyes.)* What did you do?

THÉRÈSE: Nothing.

LAURENT: And then we drifted out into the dusk, and I started to move, and what did you do?

THÉRÈSE: I watched.

LAURENT: That's right.

THÉRÈSE: You killed him, and I watched.

LAURENT: No. *WE* killed him. Say it.

THÉRÈSE: You killed him, and I watched.

LAURENT: Were you paralyzed? *(He points at* MADAME, *who looks at them with horrified contempt.)* Were you struck down too?

THÉRÈSE: You killed him, and I watched.

LAURENT: Tell me again what you said about him. When you and I lay in his bed.

THÉRÈSE: I was out of my mind.

LAURENT: You hated his sour-milk sick-room smell. You wanted to slash his pasty throat. You wanted to find a hammer, you said. And hammer his sleeping face in.

THÉRÈSE: No!

LAURENT: You did. You wanted to kill him. I wanted to kill him. We killed him.

THÉRÈSE: No...

(She starts to cry.)

LAURENT: Don't cry. DON'T CRY.

THÉRÈSE: I can cry....

LAURENT: For us.

THÉRÈSE: No. For him.

(He grabs her again.)

LAURENT: You didn't love him. You wanted him dead. We killed him.

THÉRÈSE: You killed him, and I watched.

LAURENT: NO!

THÉRÈSE: Then why does he only haunt you?

LAURENT: *Are* you out of your mind? You know you see him every night. You know if you let yourself doze for a second, he slithers right into your dreams and you wake up screaming.

THÉRÈSE: I scream because you hold on too hard. And your nails bite into my skin. In your terror.

LAURENT: I NEVER SEE HIM!

THÉRÈSE: Who?

(Unnoticed, MADAME has managed to move her hand enough to grasp the tablecloth. With a major effort of will, she yanks—and the cloth and glass and carafe come tumbling off the table.)

(LAURENT, badly startled, whirls and looks about.)

LAURENT: *(Whispered)* Camille?

THÉRÈSE: He isn't here.

(THÉRÈSE has seen that MADAME still holds an edge of the tablecloth in her lifeless hand.)

THÉRÈSE: She did it. Look.

LAURENT: She moved?

(THÉRÈSE nods. LAURENT kneels down in front of MADAME, who stares right through him.)

LAURENT: What's this? *(He pulls the cloth from her hand.)* Life in the old bat yet. Can you talk? Say something. Spit in my face. Tell me to go to hell.

(Pause)

THÉRÈSE: Where do you think you are now?

(6)

(The domino players—GRIVET, MICHAUD, OLIVIER, SUZANNE—are sitting around the immobile MADAME, at the table, playing dominoes.)

(THÉRÈSE and LAURENT sit far apart and watch.)

GRIVET: Shall I move for you, Madame?

MICHAUD: Grivet...it would be a delightful relief if you wouldn't pretend you can read her thoughts.

GRIVET: But don't I? I read her eyes, which are quite expressive. For instance— *(He holds two domino-tiles in front of* MADAME.*)* Six? Or two?

MADAME: Two. You horse's ass.

*(*GRIVET *pretends to read her face.)*

GRIVET: *Voilà!* She twinkles at six and won't look at two. So, six...*(He plays the piece.)* It's simple. My mind over her dead matter.

SUZANNE: Then what is she writing?

GRIVET: I beg your pardon?

SUZANNE: While you were gassing on and on, her fingers were tracing letters. Watch.

*(*MADAME*'s finger is shakily moving across the tablecloth.)*

*(*THÉRÈSE *and* LAURENT *sit up in fear.)*

OLIVIER: Start over again, Madame.

(She does so.)

Let's see: T...H...E...

GRIVET: *"The something..."*

SUZANNE: R...E...

GRIVET: "There but for the grace"—

MICHAUD: Hush up, Grivet!

OLIVIER: S...E...

GRIVET: "Thérèse!"

MICHAUD: Thank you, Professor.

SUZANNE: A...N...D...

MICHAUD: "Thérèse and..."

ALL THE PLAYERS: L...A...U...R...E...N...T...

GRIVET: "Thérèse and Laurent"...

ALL THE PLAYERS: A...R...E...

THÉRÈSE & LAURENT: *(Whispered)* Murderers.

(No one hears them.)

(MADAME's hand falters.)

MICHAUD: Thérèse and Laurent are...what, Madame?

SUZANNE: She's tired herself.

(MADAME's hand collapses on the table.)

GRIVET: No need for her to finish. Just look in her eyes: "Thérèse and Laurent are wonderful children, who treat me very well." Am I right?

SUZANNE: But why is she crying?

GRIVET: Gratitude.

(Pause. The game goes on.)

THÉRÈSE & LAURENT: *(Increasingly manic, as no-one hears them) Thérèse and Laurent are murderers. (Louder)* Thérèse and Laurent are murderers! *(Louder)* THÉRÈSE AND LAURENT ARE MURDERERS!

SUZANNE: Grapefruit peel?

(7)

(THÉRÈSE sits at a table, outside a cafe by the river. Night. She's drunk and wearing a simple black domino-mask that covers her eyes—as if she'd come from a masquerade ball.)

(LAURENT enters. He's also drunk and wearing a mask. He sees THÉRÈSE and approaches her table. He's carrying an artist's pad.)

LAURENT: I think I saw you, Madame—or is it Mademoiselle?

(THÉRÈSE looks over, looks away.)

LAURENT: An hour ago? At a masquerade ball.
Not far from here. By the river...

THÉRÈSE: You saw me? I don't seem to remember your
face—though the smirk is familiar.

LAURENT: Can I buy you a drink?

THÉRÈSE: The waiter's gone. He lost his nerve. The fog
is rolling off the water. See? And no one knows—

LAURENT: What?

THÉRÈSE: What's there.

(LAURENT *shivers.*)

LAURENT: Can I buy *you*?

THÉRÈSE: I'm free.

LAURENT: Even better. Come back to my garret.
I want to make love till I bleed.

THÉRÈSE: Are you an artist?

LAURENT: I am, as a matter of fact.

THÉRÈSE: You sound surprised.

LAURENT: I used to be terrible. Friends would take my
paintings down. And hang them back up when I came
to visit. But now...

(*He shows* THÉRÈSE *the sketch pad.*)

THÉRÈSE: You did these?

LAURENT: They're good. Aren't they?

THÉRÈSE: Yes. Very good. It's only.... (*She flips through
the pad.*) ...this stevedore...and this little boy, and this
dried-up crone.,.

LAURENT: Say it.

THÉRÈSE: —all look like the very same man.

LAURENT: My hand is bewitched. *(He turns the pad to a page.)* Even this kitty...

THÉRÈSE: I know that face.

LAURENT: And this dog...

THÉRÈSE: I knew a man who had this face.

LAURENT: What happened?

THÉRÈSE: He went away.

(LAURENT suddenly flings the pad offstage.)

LAURENT: People go away.

THÉRÈSE: Everything goes away. Or maybe I'm drunk.

LAURENT: You *are* drunk. And your paint is smeared all over your teeth. And you smell like an unmade bed. Did you love this man?

THÉRÈSE: I did. But not enough.

LAURENT: You left him?

THÉRÈSE: I killed him.

LAURENT: People kill people. No? Or maybe I'm drunk. I killed a man once.

THÉRÈSE: Why?

LAURENT: I wanted his wife.

THÉRÈSE: Did you get her?

LAURENT: Oh yes. We got each other. Like pox.

THÉRÈSE: And *then* what did you want?

LAURENT: Do you always want more?

THÉRÈSE: If you want the wrong things. I do.

LAURENT: I wanted peace.

THÉRÈSE: Did you get it? My guess would be—from the way the whites of your eyes are yellow, and bits of yesterday's dinner are stuck to your shirt, and your breath is rank and your hand is shaking—

LAURENT: Get up on the table. Lift your skirt. I want to fuck you.

THÉRÈSE: With what?

(Oddly, this insult makes them both laugh. THÉRÈSE gets onto the table, and cradles LAURENT with her legs.)

LAURENT: Hold on: I'm not hard.

THÉRÈSE: You aren't dead.

(They laugh again.)

LAURENT: You cunt.

THÉRÈSE: You seeping prick. Fuck me.

LAURENT: I can't.

THÉRÈSE: I don't want you to. Fuck me.

LAURENT: I CAN'T!

THÉRÈSE: I DON'T WANT YOU TO. FUCK ME!

LAURENT: I can't.

THÉRÈSE: I don't want you. Hold me close.

(Pause. LAURENT stares at her.)

LAURENT: I can't.

(With a final look of regret at THÉRÈSE, he exits. She watches him go.)

(8)

(MADAME and THÉRÈSE, alone at the table.)

(THÉRÈSE gets up from her chair and sits at the feet of MADAME.)

MADAME: When you lean against me...Thérèse?
Can you hear me? No...

THÉRÈSE: I'm pregnant now. I don't think it's a baby,
though. I think it's somebody who drowned. A baby
would ride the waves and float. But this thing inside
me is under water. I feel it decomposing. Cold and
soft...I haven't told Laurent. Tonight, when we fight,
I'll drive him mad. I know how. I'll say that I never
loved him. Ever. I'll say that I only loved Camille. But
not enough. I'll say—ohmigod...I'll say he's turning *into*
Camille. He'll beat me up. It helps him sleep. It helps *me*
sleep. You're turning into Camille, I'll say. Your flesh
has crumbled. You glow in the dark like rot. He'll beat
me harder than ever tonight. The baby will go away.
(She takes MADAME's *hand, holds it to her own cheek.)*
I loved your son. I sent him to his death.... If you could
forgive me, I'd kill myself and end in peace.

MADAME: When you lean against me...Thérèse?...
I almost believe in God again, because, when you lean
against me, whining your hypocritical speeches, crying
your crocodile tears, killing my son again and again, I
think I am being tortured and beg for death but I never
die, and someone allows this torture. That must be God.

*(*THÉRÈSE *looks up at* MADAME, *as* LAURENT *enters.)*

LAURENT: Get off the floor. *(*THÉRÈSE *doesn't move.)*
GET OFF THE FLOOR!

*(*THÉRÈSE *gets up. She whispers to* MADAME.*)*

THÉRÈSE: *Do* you forgive me?

LAURENT: SHE FORGIVES YOU. She wishes she'd had
a dozen children. So you could have killed them all too.

*(*THÉRÈSE *ignores* LAURENT.*)*

THÉRÈSE: He was so good.

LAURENT: So good he couldn't speak one silly word without grating your nerves.

THÉRÈSE: I loved him.

LAURENT: Not all of him, though. Not his softness, remember? You used to beat on my chest when you came. And you thanked me for being so hard. And solid. You said when you had to touch him, your fingers sank into his flesh like dough.

(With sudden determination, THÉRÈSE *begins to exit.)*

(He stops her.)

LAURENT: Where are you going?

THÉRÈSE: To the police. I want this over.

(He stares at her. Then he thrusts her away.)

LAURENT: Then go.

(But she hesitates. He watches her and makes a decision.)

LAURENT: *I'll* go. *(He starts to exit, then stops.)*

(They stare at each other.)

*(*CAMILLE *enters and sits at the table, near his mother, who doesn't see him.)*

*(*LAURENT *and* THÉRÈSE *don't look at* CAMILLE.*)*

THÉRÈSE: He's here.

LAURENT: I know.

THÉRÈSE: For good. *(Pause)* At first I thought he was already here.

LAURENT: What do you mean?

THÉRÈSE: Just now, when you came in, I thought you were him.

(Water begins to trickle, then stream out of CAMILLE's *mouth.)*

(No one moves.)

CAMILLE: Tonight, when he beats you...you'll turn to meet his kicks. *(To* LAURENT:*)* She'll rake your neck, where the mark of my teeth is burning on down to the bone. You won't be responsible...

(To THÉRÈSE*)* You'll let him kick you, until you think you'll die.

THÉRÈSE: Will the baby live? *(*CAMILLE *doesn't answer.)* Could the baby have lived?

(Silence.)

LAURENT: I have a chemist friend. I said we have rats. He's promised me a bottle of prussic acid.

THÉRÈSE: I've been sharpening a kitchen knife.

CAMILLE: I won't tell.

(9)

(The river)

*(*MADAME—*in a high-backed wheelchair—is being pushed by* LAURENT *to the bank of the river.* THÉRÈSE *comes after, lugging a basket.)*

MADAME: Why stop here? Below a rotting bridge, in shadow—oh. In shadow: because you're ashamed. Picnic by the sewer—nice. With the water lapping the dead fish up, and the empty bottles of sour wine, and isn't that somebody's used French letter? Bobbing. Cold dead seed...

THÉRÈSE: *(Looking about)* Here?

LAURENT: No.

THÉRÈSE: Why not?

(Pause)

LAURENT: Why not?

(Below MADAME, LAURENT *sits down.* THÉRÈSE *sits down beside him, putting the basket between then.)*

THÉRÈSE: I used to lie down by the river. Doze in the sun. When I was a girl—

LAURENT: You were never a girl. You said.

(Pause)

THÉRÈSE: Sometimes, when the wind would kick up the water, I liked to pretend the river was going to leap its banks and attack me. My heart would pound, my muscles would tense, I'd try to think how to fight back...

LAURENT: Were you happy? *(No answer)* You said when you met me you wanted to tear me apart. *(No response)* Did you ever love me?

THÉRÈSE: Yes.

LAURENT: I loved you.

(Pause) After I killed him—

THÉRÈSE: *We* killed him.

LAURENT: That's right. After we killed him, before we married... I'd wander the streets. I couldn't sleep. One night the rain fell in great waves and I slid my way down the embankment here, to take shelter under this bridge. I must have been crouched in this place for hours. Till dawn. Things drifted down the river. Shapes...I thought, if I ever escaped from this place, you could save me—

THÉRÈSE: From what?

LAURENT: The voices in the water.

(Pause)

THÉRÈSE: Do you want some wine?

LAURENT: Don't you?

(She reaches into the basket, pulls out a bottle and hands it to him.)

(With his back to her, he pulls the cork—and then he takes a small vial from out of his pocket, pouring part of the contents into the bottle of wine.)

(While LAURENT *is doping the wine,* THÉRÈSE *reaches into the basket, extracting a long sharp kitchen knife.)*

*(*MADAME *is watching all this with the greatest interest.)*

*(With their backs to each other—him holding the vial, her holding the knife—*LAURENT *begins to speak.)*

LAURENT: Take off your shoe.

Let me kiss your foot.
Let me taste your skin.
Let me hear your blood.
Let me kiss you.
Let me put my tongue in you.
Let me bury my face.
Let me smell you.
Let me hide.
End me.
Thérèse.

THÉRÈSE: We did all that. Before we killed Camille. Before we died.

(At that moment they slowly turn to face each other.)

(She sees the vial of poison; he sees the knife. Pause.)

LAURENT: Do it.

THÉRÈSE: No. You.

*(*THÉRÈSE *puts down the knife.)*

(As if hypnotized, LAURENT *pours the rest of the vial into the bottle of wine.)*

(Then he puts the bottle down.)

(They stare at each other.)

(Then they embrace, with great passion and greater tenderness.)

(Finally, they break apart.)

(LAURENT *drinks from the bottle, letting it spill ecstatically over his face and head.)*

(He hands the bottle to THÉRÈSE. *She drinks with the same abandon, soaking herself.)*

(THÉRÈSE *and* LAURENT *look at each other.)*

MADAME: What will I say, when they find me?
If they find me...
Somebody will find me, sooner or later,
I don't mind waiting....
Your bodies will teem with maggots,
dogs will bark at your carcasses,
someone will complain of the smell
below this bridge.
I don't mind waiting....
When I was a girl a summer night
was like an open wound,
hot, sticky, wet...sweet—
my husband put his hand inside
and hurt my heart.
I had a child.
You killed him....
I hear him,
standing in the current,
watching you lie where you fell,
Laurent, Thérèse,
you twitch, you twitch a final time,
you stop, and then—
when he's certain you're still...
I know he will come,

stepping out of the river,
shining wet and
happy at last.
I don't mind waiting.
(Long pause. MADAME *looks out, uncertain.)*
Camille?

(As THÉRÈSE *and* LAURENT *regard each other, and*
MADAME *waits for* CAMILLE—*who doesn't appear—*
the lights fade to black.)

CURTAIN